YOUR KNOWLEDGE HAS VALUE

- We will publish your bachelor's and master's thesis, essays and papers

- Your own eBook and book - sold worldwide in all relevant shops

- Earn money with each sale

Upload your text at www.GRIN.com and publish for free

Bibliographic information published by the German National Library:

The German National Library lists this publication in the National Bibliography; detailed bibliographic data are available on the Internet at http://dnb.dnb.de .

Imprint:

Copyright © 2014 GRIN Verlag
Print and binding: Books on Demand GmbH, Norderstedt Germany
ISBN: 9783656903628

This book at GRIN:

https://www.grin.com/document/293078

Franz-Joseph Reisner

Can the Eurozone survive?

Potential prospects for the Euro as common currency beyond the sovereign-debt crisis

GRIN Verlag

GRIN - Your knowledge has value

Since its foundation in 1998, GRIN has specialized in publishing academic texts by students, college teachers and other academics as e-book and printed book. The website www.grin.com is an ideal platform for presenting term papers, final papers, scientific essays, dissertations and specialist books.

Visit us on the internet:

http://www.grin.com/

http://www.facebook.com/grincom

http://www.twitter.com/grin_com

CAN THE EUROZONE SURVIVE?

POTENTIAL PROSPECTS FOR THE EURO AS COMMON

CURRENCY BEYOND THE SOVEREIGN-DEBT CRISIS

Franz-Joseph Reisner

Table of contents

Index of Abbreviations 2

Introduction..3

Analysing the past...3

The Present: Contributing factors and relevant players.......................................5

Future expectations beyond the sovereign-debt crisis 8

Conclusion... 10

Bibliography... 11

Appendix.. 12

Index of Abbreviations

EC	European Community
ECB	European Central Bank
EMI	European Monetary Institute
EMU	Economic and Monetary Union
ERM	Exchange Rate Mechanism
ESCB	European System of Central Banks
ESFS	European Financial Stability Facility
ESM	European Stability Mechanism
EU	European Union
GDP	Gross Domestic Product
GDR	German Democratic Republic (East Germany)
IMF	International Monetary Fund
LTRO	long term refinancing operation
OECD	Organisation for Economic Cooperation and Development
OMT	outright monetary transactions
OPEC	Organisation of the Petroleum Exporting Countries
SGP	Stability and Growth Pact

Introduction

This report critically evaluates and addresses the past, current and the possible future situation of the Eurozone. Intended politically as the major contribution to a United Europe, and perceived by many at the time of its introduction as an enormous accomplishment, "The Euro, probably more than any other currency, represents the mutual confidence at the heart of our community" (Wim Duisenberg, President of the ECB in 2002, quoted in Marsh, 2009, p.1). Yet, roughly a decade after Duisenberg´s speech, much of this euphoria has dampened as the Eurozone continues to struggle with the impacts of the economic crisis of 2008. Indeed, little of Duisenberg's claimed ´mutual confidence´ remained after Greece went effectively bankrupt and bondholders had to accept a €100 billion ´haircut´ in early 2012. Moreover, the risk of contagion from Greece to the economies of Portugal, Ireland, Italy and Spain (commonly referred to as periphery countries or PIIGS, see appendix) and the extensive discourse of "Grexit", a Greek exit from the common European currency, have increasingly complicated the current situation. To consider the question of whether the Eurozone will be able to survive, the first part of this report provides an overview of past developments regarding the Euro, and how the Euro's complex history has led to the current situation, including potentially contributing factors to the crisis. The second part then focuses on the present situation: Greece causing the potential threat of a rapid domino effect that could splinter the Eurozone as a whole. Subsequently, this report evaluates if the measures, imposed by the EU, ECB and IMF will be adequate to finally resolve the crisis, before focusing on the potential future of the Euro as a common currency for Europe.

Analysing the past

The creation of the Euro has its origins in the early 1970s collapse of post-war Bretton Woods agreement (see appendix) (Lucarelli, 2013; Chabot, 1999). The subsequent following exchange-rate volatility as well as the oil price shocks (a sudden quadrupling of the oil prices by the OPEC cartel in mid-1973) led to relatively high inflation rates and resulted in a strong European desire for a zone of monetary stability (Lucarelli, 2013). Hence, in 1979, the European Community introduced the Exchange Rate Mechanism (ERM, see appendix) that tied the 'weaker' European currencies to the relatively stable Deutschmark (Roscini & Schlefer, 2013). In 1986 the EC signed the Single European Act (see appendix) as a pledge to systematically abandon trade barriers, border checks, tariffs, and also financial and labour restrictions (Bishop, et al., 1996).

Many then argued that a single trans-European currency would be the logical consequence, both for a lasting peace in Europe as well as the economic benefits of free trade and monetary stability (Chabot, 1999). Arguably, forming a single currency union was seen as the most effective way to cement 40 years of international cooperation and peace in Europe, the objectives were therefore political as much as economic (Roscini & Schlefer, 2013). German Chancellor Helmut Kohl emphasised in 1997 that "the bitter experiences of war and dictatorship in this century teach us that the unification project is the best insurance against a relapse of national egoism, chauvinism and violent conflict" (Chabot, 1999, p. 38). This emphasis on political hopes of several participating countries and the deeply held aspirations represented a major difference to any other previous currency blueprint. Additionally, ambitious economic goals, such as eradicating exchange rate volatility, enhancing price transparency and decreasing transaction costs also played a significant role (Chabot, 1999).

The Maastricht Treaty (see appendix) officially formed the EU in 1992 and laid the groundwork for the European Central Bank (ECB) (Bishop, et al., 1996; Chabot, 1999). On 1 January, 1999 six (of the original 11) Eurozone members did not actually adhere to the Maastricht criteria (see appendix), yet were able to join the Eurozone and, in practice, some members only attained the Maastricht criteria through 'creative accounting'. Furthermore, the Stability and Growth Pact (SGP, see appendix) was often unheeded as several member countries violated both debt and deficit levels (Arestis & Sawyer, 2012).

With the adoption of the Euro as a common currency the euro members discontinued their own individual monetary policies, yet remained autonomous with their fiscal policies. Arestis and Sawyer (2012) point out, that this may be seen as a key flaw within the Treaty and a major reason for the sovereign-debt crisis. Before implementing the Euro, Eurozone countries were able to respond to economic shocks and crisis through three options: (1) adjustment of interest rates; (2) exchange rate adjustment, hence devaluation of the currency and (3) fiscal adjustment, hence government spending and taxes (Chabot, 1999). All Eurozone members surrendered the first two mechanisms, and with this a considerable degree of autonomy, to the ECB. This resulted in a severely limited scope for the national governments regarding countercyclical policies (Lucarelli, 2013). Arestis and Sawyer (2012, p. 29) point out that without the ability to devalue the currencies, countries with high current account deficits "will be thrown back into deflation". This becomes particularly clear given that the Maastricht Treaty demanded that governments that had borrowed more than 60% of GDP had to impose a restrictive fiscal policy, even if these measures would intensify a potential recession (Lucarelli, 2013).

The Present: Contributing factors and relevant players

This section will provide an overview of contributing factors to the current crisis. In particular, the weaknesses and turbulences of the financial markets will be discussed before addressing the changed conditions in relevant countries since the monetary unification.

Before adopting the euro investors demanded higher interest rates, or "inflation and exchange rate risk premiums", from the peripheral countries (Chabot, 1999, p. 46). The Euro lowered inflation and eliminated exchange rate risks and therefore countries with a historically high inflation (PIIGS, see appendix) benefited enormously from the downward pressure of interest rates on their government bonds (Chabot, 1999). This increasing confidence led to significantly lower "risk premiums" and encouraged institutional and private investors to pour capital into the periphery countries (Roscini & Schlefer, 2013). Following a common macroeconomic sense (Blanchard, 2011), an increase in government spending contributes to an overall increase in demand and deficit spending of periphery governments skyrocketed after adopting the Euro (Roscini & Schlefer, 2013). Figure 1 (Lucarelli, 2013) illustrates the alignment of European ten-year government bonds and highlights the harmonization of the spread between the currency unification 1999 and the Lehman Bankruptcy 2008.

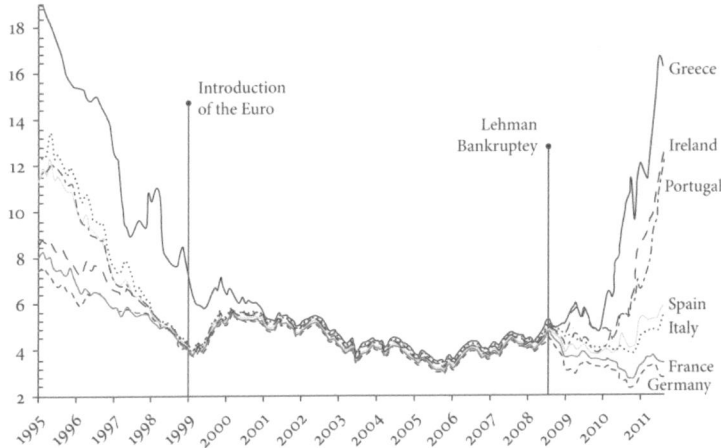

FIGURE 1   *Interest rates on 10-year government bonds (%)*
Source: Bill Lucarelli; *Endgame for the Euro*; p. 132

According to some research, European banks had operated with huge leverage since the early 2000s (Roscini & Schlefer, 2013; Lucarelli, 2013). A strong exposure to mortgage-backed securities and other toxic assets made many banks highly vulnerable to the implications of the US housing bubble, that rapidly evolved to a financial crisis and spread to a global economic crisis (Lucarelli, 2013; Roscini & Schlefer, 2013). The highly leveraged and interconnected banks gave this crisis additional momentum. Subsequently, the spread on peripheral Eurozone nations' bonds diverged dramatically from the benchmark of German government bonds

(Figure 1). This in turn brought the excessive borrowing and deficit spending in the periphery to a sudden halt.

Many experts perceive the flexible labour market in Germany, reinforced by the "Agenda 2010" of former chancellor Gerhard Schröder, as the key to sustainable growth, wealth, employment and economic stability (Blum, et al., 2008). Germany was able to overcome the economic burden of the reunification with the former German Democratic Republic (GDR) and a bundle of reforms in the early 2000s allowed the improvement of industrial performance while enhancing both, the flexibility and stability that helped keep unemployment during crisis under control (Roscini & Schlefer, 2013). The peripheral countries, in contrast, relied on excessive deficit spending after adopting the euro (Lucarelli, 2013). In Greece, the budget deficit increased from 6.5% in 2007 to 15.6% of GDP in 2009 and cheap capital poured into the public sector, enabling disproportionate projects (e.g. the Athens 2004 Olympics) and the expansion of pensions (Roscini & Schlefer, 2013, Exhibit 1a). In comparison, in Spain and Ireland the capital flow fueled enormous housing bubbles, facilitated by mortgages from core European banks. Although Spanish GDP grew annually from 2000 through 2008 by only 0.7% the government debt fell continually from 59% of GDP to 40 % during the same time (Marsh, 2009; Roscini & Schlefer, 2013). The collapse of the construction sector, a result of the weakening demand for real estates since outbreak of the crisis 2008, led to an overall unemployment rate of 20% (Roscini & Schlefer, 2013). Some researchers argue that for Spain, as with Italy, the rigid labour system might have been the cause, that fiscal stimulus could not revive output once the crisis ignited (Roscini & Schlefer, 2013; Lucarelli, 2013).

However, not only Euro members were affected by the implications of the crisis. Regardless of a country's currency, implications of the sovereign-debt crisis affected all European states through closely intertwined economic and political relations. (Arestis & Sawyer, 2012) Britain and Poland, for example, two particularly relevant EU countries that are not members of the Eurozone were severely affected by the crisis. In 2012, the trade of British goods and services accounted for almost three quarters of GDP with 70% of the British export destinations within the EU (Anonymous, 2013). Poland, the most significant economy of the former communist bloc succeeded in avoiding a recession, mainly due to the domestic demand and the ability to devalue the zloty against the euro. Nonetheless, with Germany as major trade and export partner, "the nation's destiny is tied to the euro" (Anonymous, 2011).

Future expectations beyond the sovereign-debt crisis

Following the credit crunch originating from Wall Street 2008, Greece was perceived as the weakest link with a potential default causing a domino effect on the whole Eurozone. The speculation over a Greek default brought the cost of credit-default swaps (see appendix) to a peak and led major rating agencies to downgrade Greek bonds (Pryce, 2012; Lucarelli, 2013). Bond markets demanded ever higher, exorbitant interest rates as risk premiums (Figure 1) for peripheral government bonds, making the "entire eurozone [...] vulnerable to escalating bond yields" (Lucarelli, 2013, p. 131). Subsequently, in May 2010, Greece received a €110billion bail-out from the EFSM and the government implemented first austerity measures supervised by the Troika (see appendix) (Lucarelli, 2013). A week later, the IMF and EU agreed to found the European Financial Stability Facility, a €750 billion loan package from the European states, the European Commission and the IMF. In November 2010, Ireland needed a €85 billion bail-out, followed by a €78 billion bail-out package for Portugal in May 2011 (Lucarelli, 2013; Roscini & Schlefer, 2013). The European leaders agreed on the "Fiscal Compact", an adoption of tougher sanctions to further enforce the SGP, including a firm commitment to "balanced structural budgets" (Roscini & Schlefer, 2013).

By late 2011 it became clear, that Spain and Italy would be "too large for the ESFS to handle" and the Eurozone established the European Stability Mechanism (ESM), a larger, permanent rescue fund to replace the in 2013 expiring EFSF (Roscini & Schlefer, 2013, p. 8). In fall 2011, Greece applied for a second € 130 billion bail-out and private bondholders agreed to take a 50% 'haircut' (Pryce, 2012).

To provide liquidity to banks, ECB-President Mario Draghi offered a "wall of money" (an unlimited volume of low interest-rate loans with three years maturity), referred to as "long term refinancing operation"(LTRO) that increased total ECB lending to more than €3 trillion (Roscini & Schlefer, 2013). In 2012 the Eurozone finance ministers agreed to a €100 billion bank rescue package to recapitalise Spanish banks (Roscini & Schlefer, 2013; Lucarelli, 2013).

By spring 2012, it was obvious that Europe still was not growing and the human cost of the austerity measures in recent years had been enormous for the periphery states (Arestis & Sawyer, 2012). In July 2012, at the euro crisis´ peak, the surging yields for Spanish and Italian bonds threatened the further existence of the common currency. To counter rumors of a "Grexit" and the breakup of the 17-nation currency bloc, Mario Draghi gave a courageous promise, "to do whatever it takes to preserve the euro" and reassured that "it will be enough" (Lucarelli, 2013, p. 14). The ECB´s "outright monetary transactions" (OMT) enabled the intervention in surging bond markets to prevent "unjustifiably high interest rates" (Roscini & Schlefer, 2013, p. 14). This marked a turning point, and confidence returned to financial markets. Nonetheless, on 25 June 2012 Cyprus, closely intertwined with struggling Greece, asked for a bail-out (Roscini & Schlefer, 2013).

The historically low interest rates as well as the implemented measures of EU,ECB and IMF were, up to the present day, not sufficient enough to sustainably revive growth in the Eurozone and the fear of recession is still prevalent (Darvas, 2013; Lucarelli, 2013).

Those facts intensify the questions of whether the Eurozone can survive and, bearing the flaws of the monetary union in mind, whether it should survive? Arguably, the Eurozone economies had not converged and did not converge through the adoption of a single currency. Lucarelli (2013) concludes that the endurance of the euro-system in its current form appears to be increasingly problematic. Arestis and Sawyer (2012, p. 30) point out, that "in the absence of economic integration, a monetary union without a political integration simply cannot survive". Arguably, the long-term resolution lays in surrendering the fiscal autonomy of the member states. Furthermore, the fate of the euro depends on the willingness of Germany to fund the deficit countries and carry a major share of the debt (Arestis & Sawyer, 2012). Eventually, more debt will need to be written off and expansionary fiscal policies have to be extended across the Eurozone to "counter-act potential economic stagnation and re-activate growth" (Lucarelli, 2013, p. 137).

Conclusion

It is arguably clear, that the adoption of the euro as a common currency had numerous advantages for all member countries. Nonetheless, the profound difficulties of the euro crisis cast a dark shadow over the future of the common currency. Considering the severe austerity measures imposed on the periphery countries poses the question of how long they will be able to bear the burden of ongoing austerity. As many countries suffer from the current situation, higher levels of investment would make a better contribution to reduce budget deficits, rather than solely focusing on fiscal austerity. However, even with the support of ECB, EU and IMF, the disparities in economic performance among the member states will continue to be persistent. Nonetheless, being part of a vibrant, competitive and growing Europe is in each Eurozone country's political and economic long-term interest. By bearing its initial political and economic objectives in mind, the Eurozone clearly should survive and if the member countries are willing to make substantial contributions and further concessions, such as to surrender their fiscal autonomy, the Eurozone can survive.

Reference list

Anonymous, 2011. "Look at it this way; Non-members", *The Economist (US),* Volume 401.8759, Print Edition, Nov. 12, 2011, p. 13.

Anonymous, 2012. "Europe´s Achilles heel: the Euro crisis", *The Economist (US),* Volume 403.8784, p. 11.

Anonymous, 2013. "An island of traders", *The Economist (Britain),* Print Edition, May 18 ,2013 p.31.

Arestis, P. & Sawyer, M., 2012. *The Euro Crisis.* Houndmills, Hampshire: Palgrave Macmillan.

Bishop, G., Pérez, J. & van Tuyll, S., 1996. *User Guide to the Euro.* London: The Federal Trust for Education and Research.

Blanchard, O., 2011. *Macroeconomics.* 5th ed.; Boston, MA: Pearson Education.

Blum, U. et al., 2008. "Agenda 2010 - Eine Zwischenbilanz", *Wirtschaftsdienst,* Volume 3, pp. 151-152.

Chabot, C. N., 1999. *Understanding the euro: the clear and concise guide to the new trans-european economy.* New York: McGraw-Hill.

Darvas, Z., 2013. "The Euro Crisis: Mission Accomplished?" *World Policy Journal,* Volume 30(1), pp. 87-94.

Lucarelli, B., 2013. *Endgame for the Euro: a critical history.* Basingstoke: Palgrave Macmillan.

Marsh, D., 2009. *The euro: the politics of the new global currency.* New Haven, CT: Yale University Press.

Pryce, V., 2012. *Greekonomics.* London: Biteback Publishing Ltd.

Roscini, D. & Schlefer, J., 2013. *Can the Eurozone Survive?,* Boston, MA: Harvard Business School.

Appendix

Bretton Woods system: A system of monetary management established in 1944, that fixed the United States dollar against gold and other currencies against the dollar. It established the rules for commercial and financial relations among the world's major industrial states in the mid-twentieth century.

Credit default swap: CDS is a financial swap agreement, where the seller of the CDS will compensate the buyer in the event of a loan default or other credit event. The buyer of the CDS makes a series of payments to the seller and, in exchange, receives a payoff if the loan defaults.

Dept-to-GDP ratio: The amount of national debt of a country as a percentage of its gross domestic product (GDP) and one of the indicators of the health of an economy.

Eurozone: An economic and monetary union (EMU) of European Union (EU) member states that have adopted the euro (€) as their common currency and sole legal tender.

Exchange Rate Mechanism   The ERM had the objectives of stabilizing currencies and lowering inflation rates by tying the ´weaker´ European currencies to the relatively stable Deutschmark.

Maastricht Treaty: Formally the Treaty on European Union, signed on 7 February 1992 by the members of the European Community in Maastricht, the Netherlands. The treaty officially formed the EU and the European System of

Central Banks (ESCB), consisting of the ECB and the national central banks of the member states. Among other things, the Maastricht "convergence" criteria for adopting the euro are a fiscal deficit below 3% of GDP as well as a government debt limit of 60% of GDP.

Member state:
A state that is party to treaties of the European Union (EU) and thereby subject to the privileges and obligations of EU membership.

PIIGS:
The term describing Portugal, Ireland, Italy, Greece and Spain (also referred to as the "periphery states").

Private sector involvement PSI refers to the participation of the private sector in the write downs of sovereign-debt in instances of "haircut".

Single European Act:
SEA, the first major revision of the 1957 Treaty of Rome. The Act set the objective of establishing a single market by 31 December 1992, and codified European Political Co-operation, the forerunner of the European Union´s Common Foreign and Security Policy.

Stability and Growth Pact:
SPG, An agreement made by the twenty-seven member states of the EU, to facilitate and maintain the stability of the Economic and Monetary Union.

Treaty of Rome:
The treaty signed in 1957 establishing the European Economic Community (EEC) as a customs union on 1 January 1958.

Troika:
refers to the committee of European Commission, European Central Bank and the International Monetary Fund.

\